Today the experience of Paris from and beside the S[...] a fascination than Lowell spoke of more than a h[...] although his *bateaux mouches* were the passenger [...] by the engines manufactured at la Mouche, a district of L[...] name is that of one of the four cruise boat companies that offer the visitor what is, perhaps, the best introduction to this jewel of a city.

There are attractive alternatives. The map suggests the Batobus (in the tourist season a scheduled riverbus service), the two regular bus routes (24 and 72) that serve the length of the Seine from the Pont Sully in the east to the Pont de Grenelle in the west, and the Métro and RER trains. For bargain travel, ask at a Métro or RER station for details of the Paris Visite card – it is good for the bus and other conveyances as well as for trains. At the same time consider buying a museums pass (carte inter-musées) – museum visitors can make big savings and avoid the queues.

For those who are able, the most satisfying way to explore Paris is on foot. A recommended walking route is shown, and the berges, the banks close to the water, are a welcome relief from the bustle of the quais above. In the evening the pleasure experienced by Lowell is enhanced today by the illumination of every major monument along the river.

However you choose to explore Paris by the Seine, one thing is certain: the memories will last a lifetime.

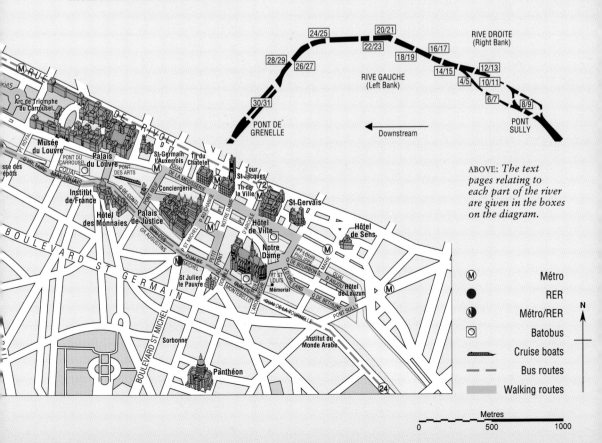

ABOVE: *The text pages relating to each part of the river are given in the boxes on the diagram.*

ABOVE: *The distinctive spire and roof of the Sainte-Chapelle can be glimpsed within the embracing solidity of the Palais de Justice.*

RIGHT: *The Sainte-Chapelle is a wonder of Gothic architecture, the walls appearing to consist almost entirely of stained glass.*

ABOVE: *From the Pont des Arts the Ile de la Cité seems tethered in the stream by the twin ties of the Pont-Neuf. The evening sun catches the dome of the Institut de France.*

RIGHT ABOVE: *Atop the quayside walls are the lock-up booths of the 'bouquinistes' – the booksellers trading in everything from posters and postcards through literature to obscure academic tomes.*

RIGHT BELOW: *The grotesques carved on the Pont-Neuf recall the hucksters who traded here in the 17th century.*

T he Pont-Neuf – the New Bridge
– is now the oldest in Paris. It
was inaugurated by Henri IV
riding across in 1605. He created a fresh centre to the city, for his
bridge was wide open, free of houses and
with the new idea of raised sidewalks for
pedestrians. It soon became thronged,
according to Bethod, with charlatans, ras-
cals, booksellers, singers, cut-purses, physi-
cians, jugglers and chicken-vendors. The
statue of Henri IV surveys passers-by on
the bridge. It is a replacement of the original of 1613 which was melted down in
1792 to provide cannon for the Revolutionary armies. In 1818 the replacement was
cast from melted statues of Napoleon.
Behind the statue, at the western end of the
island is the Square du Vert-Galant.
Named for Henri in tribute to his energy
and vivacity, it is a peaceful and shady
haven for the footsore sightseer.

On the southern bank of the island is
the Quai des Orfèvres (Goldsmiths) where,
at No 36, Simenon's Inspector Maigret had
his headquarters, as do the real life 'flics',
the Police Judiciaire, today. Rising above
the Palais de Justice is the slender spire of
the Sainte-Chapelle. St Louis built this

shrine for the Crown of Thorns, finishing
it in 1248. By the time of the Revolution it
had become a warehouse for flour and in
1837 it still bore the sign 'National prop-
erty: For Sale'. Its restoration was part of
the massive works undertaken by Haussmann and his architect Viollet-le-Duc in
the 19th century.

On the left bank is the Quai des Grands-
Augustins. Near the river, the bouquinistes;
opposite, fine houses of the 16th, 17th and
18th centuries occupy the site of the
Augustinian monastery from which the
modern name comes.

RIGHT: *Floodlighting emphasises the splendour of Notre-Dame, the first of France's great Gothic cathedrals. The east end, with its flying buttresses, was completed in 1345.*

FAR RIGHT: *The numerous little old streets of the left bank are full of interest for the visitor. Here an instant portrait artist on the Pont au Double both entertains and creates a unique souvenir.*

BELOW: *Notre-Dame is famous for its carved stone gargoyles. The spire, which was destroyed in the Revolution, was rebuilt by 19th-century restorer Viollet-le-Duc who included himself amongst the copper figures of the saints.*

The Pont St Michel, built in 1857 when the maze of unhealthy streets on the left bank was swept away to form the Place St Michel, is on the site of a bridge built in 1378 and is the fifth to stand here. The Petit-Pont occupies the site of the earliest bridge of all, that built by the Romans. It was for years the only bridge to the south, guarded on the bank by the Petit-Châtelet, a fortified gatehouse and prison first in wood and rebuilt in stone in 1369 to last for four centuries. Opening on the quay to the west of the Petit-Pont is the Rue du Chat-qui-Pêche, the narrowest in Paris at 2.5 metres (8 feet 3 ins). Behind the Quai de Montebello and off Square Viviani, where stands the church of St Julien-le-Pauvre, one of the oldest (1240) in Paris, runs the Rue de la Bûcherie, dating from the early 13th century.

Notre-Dame has witnessed innumerable historic events over the centuries. Henry VI of England was crowned here in 1430. Here Mary Queen of Scots celebrated her marriage to François II, as Henri IV did his to Marguerite de Valois, though, as a Protestant, he stood outside the cathedral during the service. Although Napoleon had himself crowned here, the building was actually sold, incredibly, to a demolition contractor. It was eventually saved largely through the influence of a single person, Victor Hugo, whose tale of the Hunchback in his long novel, Notre-Dame de Paris, revived respect for the great monument.

ABOVE: *Within the eastern tip of the island a stark sculpture forms part of the Memorial to the Deportation. Tiny lights commemorate many thousands of French victims of Nazism.*

LEFT: *Visitors crowd the Parvis below the west front of Notre-Dame. In the Middle Ages the numerous statues were brightly coloured and stood in gilded niches, a Bible in stone.*

ABOVE: *The ornate down-pipe of the façade of the Hôtel Lauzun hints at the magnificence of the 17th-century style of decoration within.*

RIGHT: *Almost hidden on the right bank stands a medieval château, the Hôtel de Sens, once the residence of the Archbishop of Sens, ecclesiastical overlord of Paris until 1623.*

FAR LEFT: Winter floods cover the banks below the Quai d'Anjou and the leafless trees permit a view of the fine houses fronting the river.

LEFT: Summer warmth, and there's no finer thing to do than enjoy a bottle of wine with a friend on the Quai d'Orleans.

BELOW: The Quai d'Anjou. In the 1850s the poet Baudelaire had an apartment at the Hôtel Lauzun where the Hashish Club welcomed Delacroix, Daumier, Balzac, Sickert, Rilke and Wagner among others.

O n the left bank the Quai de la Tournelle runs where 'la Tournelle', the fort that protected this flank of Paris, stood until 1790. On the modern bridge the statue of St Genevieve is artistically placed off-centre, under the eyes of the diners at La Tour d'Argent. Further east, facing the Pont Sully, stands the Institut du Monde Arabe, a marvel of modern architecture.

The Quais of the Ile St Louis offer some of the most pleasant walking in Paris or a place to read, eat a picnic, or just sit with the one you love and watch the world go by. The island is a living example of 17th-century town planning, based on a grid system with the great houses (hôtels) facing the river and the shops on a long straight street down the centre.

On the southern side of the island are the houses favoured by the rich and famous of our day, keen to enjoy the sun. Marie Curie lived at 8, Quai d'Orléans. Sheltered from a peasant sun-tan on the northern side, the finest houses are found. On the Quai d'Anjou the Hôtel Lambert's rear windows overlook its gardens and the river. A small wall-plaque commemorates Daumier's residence at 9 and at 17 the sober façade of the Hôtel de Lauzun is half-concealed by the trees.

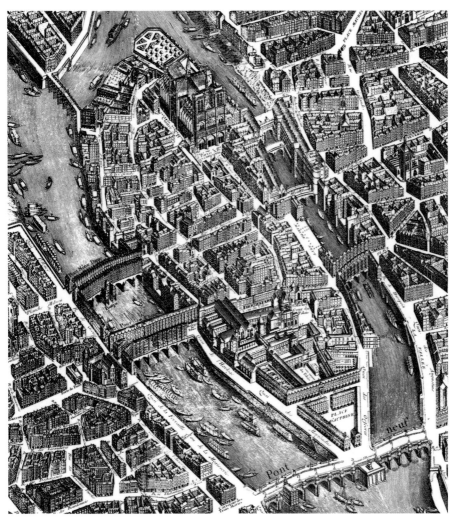

LEFT: *The Ile de la Cité as shown on Turgot's map of Paris, dating from 1740. The north is to the left, the east at the top. The north-eastern quarter of the island is still very close to this plan; the Rue Chanoinesse can be traced by romantics with thoughts of Abélard and Héloïse. The schemes of Haussmann spared only the Conciergerie and Sainte-Chapelle to the west.*

Most bridges are heavy with houses and the quays are built over as well; a view of the river from a street was most unusual.

On the Pont-Neuf, close to the right bank, stands la Samaritaine. Until 1813 this was a water pumping station, named after the woman of Samaria who gave Jesus water. The name was 'borrowed' for the modern department store nearby, and from its rooftop café something close to this view can be enjoyed.

RIGHT: *They are not forgotten. After more than forty-five years fresh flowers are still placed on this memorial to a hero of the Liberation.*

The Pont Notre-Dame is on the site of the ancient Grand Pont which was burnt by the Normans, the Viking invaders of Normandy, in 887. The Pont au Change acquired its name as, in the 13th century, its houses were occupied by gold and silversmiths and by moneylenders, thus 'Pont au Changeurs' and, eventually, Pont au Change.

To the west of the Pont au Change stands the massive façade of the Conciergerie, built by Philip the Fair in the early 14th century. The name Conciergerie was given to that part of a palace occupied by the nobleman responsible for the safekeeping of the royal residence, and thus has links with the more humble calling of the concierge of a modern apartment house.

It ceased to be a palace after only 50 years, when Charles V favoured the Louvre, and the lasting fame of the Conciergerie is as a prison. The unlucky Montgomery, captain of Henri II's guard, who killed his sovereign in a joust in 1559, was held here before his execution, and the application of torture to successive unfortunates gave rise to the name of the western tower overlooking the river – Bonbec, the babbler.

During the Revolution these grim surroundings gave all-too-temporary shelter to over 2,500 victims destined for the guillotine; Marie-Antoinette, Charlotte Corday, Mme du Barry, Danton and Robespierre among them. A visit to the Conciergerie's museum and to the cells provides a vivid picture of those troubled times.

ABOVE LEFT: *In the Place Louis-Lépine off the Quai de Corse is the flower market; on Sundays a market for songbirds.*

TOP: *From the Pont au Change to the Pont-Neuf runs the Quai de l'Horloge, overlooked by the walls and towers of the Conciergerie.*

ABOVE: *Overlooking the Pont au Change in a square tower is l'Horloge – Paris's first public clock, which has kept time here since 1370.*

ABOVE: *The Hôtel de Ville was built in neo-Renaissance style to replace the building burnt down in 1871 during the Commune. The exterior is generously furnished with statues of allegorical figures and prominent historical personages.*

ABOVE RIGHT: *The Place de l'Hôtel de Ville was known, until 1830, as the Place de Grève. It was formerly a gently sloping foreshore (grève) to the Seine where cargoes were landed and longshoremen gathered in hope of employment. Thus 'faire la grève' meant to be unemployed, then 'en grève' came to mean on strike.*

RIGHT: *The Tour St Jacques, all that remains of the 16th-century church of St-Jacques-la-Boucherie from which pilgrims set out on their journey to the shrine of Santiago de Compostela in northern Spain.*

From the river little more than the tower of the church of St-Gervais-St-Protais can be seen on the right bank, but on foot the full extravagance of this 17th-century Gothic basilica can be appreciated. The church is dedicated to the two Roman soldiers martyred by the Emperor Nero.

The Place de Grève, now the Place de l'Hôtel de Ville, was the scene of public executions, many of them horribly slow to punish the crimes of treason; here perished Ravaillac, assassin of the beloved Henri IV. The area has witnessed many major events. In 1357 Etienne Marcel persuaded the hundred-year-old municipal assembly to move to the Pillared House here, and the city government has remained to this day, first in a building of the 17th century and now in the present one. The rioters took over the Hôtel de Ville after the fall of the Bastille, and it became the headquarters of the Revolutionary Commune. The rise and fall of successive regimes have

been announced here, most recently on 25 August 1944, when General de Gaulle celebrated the liberation of Paris with a crowd of 200,000 people.

The Pont au Change gives onto the Place de Châtelet on the right bank, where two theatres, built by Davioud in 1826, flank the square. In the centre stands the Palm Fountain and beyond rises the Tour St Jacques.

LEFT: *The Quai de la Mégisserie, tanners' quay. No longer the slaughterhouse district, it is filled with live animals and birds in the pet shops and green with plants for the gardener.*

ABOVE: *The Place du Châtelet, facing the Pont au Change on the right bank, was formed when the Grand–Châtelet, a great defensive gateway and prison, was demolished. The column and fountain commemorate Napoleon's victories.*

ABOVE: *The Pont des Arts, the 'academic bridge', is one of the most delightful in Paris. For pedestrians only, it is furnished with benches, and bright with flowers, and it affords a superb view. Upstream lies old Paris, downstream are the Louvre, the Tuileries gardens and, in the distance, the Grand Palais.*

The 'Academic Bridge' was built, to a novel design and all of iron, in 1803. Facing the southern end of the bridge is the Institut de France on the site of the old Hôtel de Nesle which, with its famous tower, was the western bastion of the protective fortifications of Paris.

The Tower was demolished in 1663 and, the legacy of Cardinal Mazarin, the Collège des Quatre-Nations (now the Institut de France) was built. The college was for the education of sixty scholars drawn from the 'Four Nations' of the recently acquired provinces of the kingdom. During the Reign of Terror the Committee of Public Safety sat here, sending hundreds to the guillotine. In 1805 Napoleon assigned the buildings to the Institut de France, of which the constituent Academies are those of Fine Arts, Inscriptions and Belles Lettres, Science, Moral and Political Sciences and, of course, the world renowned Académie française.

Adjacent to the Institut, facing the Quai de Conti and the floating headquarters of the river fire service, is the Mint, the Hôtel des Monnaies.

LEFT: *Although the 'Immortals' of the Académie française pass through these dignified portals, the Institut de France displays a modest street number.*

TOP: *Designed by Louis Le Vau to harmonize with the Louvre across the river, the curved wings and the dome of the Institut de France pay homage to scholarship.*

ABOVE: *An artist takes advantage of the view from the Pont des Arts; the Ile de la Cité and the Quai de Conti are blocked in on canvas.*

ABOVE: *Of the Palace of the Tuileries only Le Nôtre's gardens survive, but here one can stroll, take refreshment, relax in the shade and children can sail boats on the pond.*

RIGHT: *The last remnants of the Louvre as a fortification can be seen in this 17th-century painting by Verwer. By night a chain from the 'Porte Neuve' – New Gate – to the Tour de Nesle closed the river. In the distance the Pont-Neuf, and everywhere people, boats, horses and coaches.*

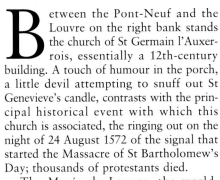

B etween the Pont-Neuf and the Louvre on the right bank stands the church of St Germain l'Auxerrois, essentially a 12th-century building. A touch of humour in the porch, a little devil attempting to snuff out St Genevieve's candle, contrasts with the principal historical event with which this church is associated, the ringing out on the night of 24 August 1572 of the signal that started the Massacre of St Bartholomew's Day; thousands of protestants died.

The Musée du Louvre, the world-famous art gallery, now amazes or horrifies visitors with its transition to the 'Grand Louvre', a scheme to expand the museum and to integrate it with its surroundings. In the Louvre are some of the greatest art treasures known, including the Venus de Milo, the Seated Scribe and works by Leonardo, Michaelangelo, Giotto, El Greco and Rembrandt.

The pavilion of the Orangerie, overlooking the Seine, is a pleasing little museum with works by Renoir, Modigliani, Cézanne and Matisse, as well as the renowned waterlilies by Monet.

TOP: *An unusual 140° view from the Cour Napoléon of the Louvre with Pei's dramatic Pyramid which serves as the new entrance hall and offices essential to the Grand Louvre.*

ABOVE: *Below the Quai des Tuileries the berges – banks - attract sunbathers, sometimes in an extreme state of undress. All along the Seine the berges tempt walkers, fishermen and lovers.*

ABOVE: *On a site purchased in 1897 the Orleans railway company had Victor Laloux build a new station and hotel. Redundant sixty years later, it became the Musée d'Orsay.*

RIGHT: *The conversion of the old Gare d'Orsay is deeply satisfactory, stone being used to line and develop the interior, and the facilities of the old railway station undergoing subtle modification to meet the new purpose.*

T he Quai Voltaire runs along the left bank between the Pont du Carrousel and the Pont Royal. In 1723 the writer and philosopher for whom it is named lived at the hotel at number 27, on the corner of the Rue de Beaune, east of the Pont Royal. He left because of the noise. After years of exile in Geneva he returned to this same house, only to die there a few weeks later, in February 1778.

19 Quai Voltaire, the Hôtel Voltaire, became a traveller's hotel in 1857. Here Baudelaire finished Les Fleurs du Mal, Wagner the Meistersingers and Oscar Wilde also stayed here.

For sculpture in profusion and paintings by the finest artists from 1848 to 1914, notably the Impressionists, it is to the Musée d'Orsay that one goes. In the 1960s the building was threatened with demolition. Fortunately the need for a museum to bridge the gap between the collections of the Louvre and the National Museum of Modern Art at the Pompidou Centre was recognised, and the Gare d'Orsay was designated the Musée d'Orsay. The exhibits are, generally speaking, organised chronologically, although the directional signposting leaves much to be desired. However, the richness of the collection, including many familiar paintings and pastels, sculpture, photographs and furniture, is generous compensation.

BOTTOM LEFT: *From the high terrace of the Musée d'Orsay, the Tuileries, the green-roofed Opéra and Sacré-Coeur.*

BELOW: *13 Quai Voltaire once housed Delacroix and also Corot. Ingres died at 11, the white house.*

BOTTOM RIGHT: *The decorative archway of the Caisse des Dépôts shields the courtyard from the traffic on the Quai Anatole-France and the Pont Royal. The courtyard itself provides a setting for a startling sculpture by Dubuffet.*

The Pont de la Concorde was built between 1788 and 1791 making use of dressed stone from the Bastille. It forms part of a complete sequence of buildings and thoroughfares stretching from the Palais-Bourbon on the left bank to the church of the Madeleine beyond the wide expanse of the Place de la Concorde.

To achieve this the rear of the Palais-Bourbon, the side facing the river, is provided with a corinthian colonnade to balance the façade of the Madeleine; the entrance is on the other side. The original palace on this site was built for the daughter of Louis XIV and Mme de Montespan, and had a garden next to the river. It became the meeting place of the Conseil des Cinq-Cents, the Council of the Five Hundred, the first National Assembly here, and the new building still houses the Assemblée Nationale. Further west on the Quai d'Orsay is the Ministry of Foreign Affairs, which was completed in 1857.

The Place de la Concorde's octagonal design, so well suited to the lifestyle of the

OPPOSITE ABOVE: *The Place de la Concorde is dominated by the 23 metre (75 feet) high Obélisque from Luxor. It was the gift of Mohammed Ali, the Viceroy of Egypt, in 1829.*

LEFT: *The Grand Palais was built, as was the Petit Palais facing it, for the 1900 World Exhibition. They both display the exuberant decorative style of their time.*

BELOW LEFT: *The sole survivor of the floating bath-houses of Paris, the Piscine Deligny is now a conventional swimming pool. It has been moored here since 1842.*

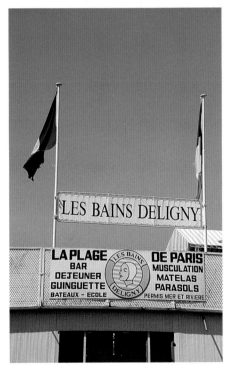

18th century stroller, was the setting for terrible events in the Reign of Terror. Richard le Gallienne tells us that here in this luminous light-hearted plaza were the headquarters of M. Sanson, the executioner, dressed in the height of fashion, with a flower in his buttonhole. Here the tumbrils packed close with fine gentlemen and fair women, surrounded by fierce-mustachioed Gardes Nationaux, unloaded their passengers, to look their haughty or mocking last through 'the little window' and 'sneeze into the basket' of sawdust.

ABOVE: *The Hôtel de Crillon is at the western end of the 18th-century mansions on the northern side of the Place de la Concorde. The entrance faced the guillotine, close to the statue symbolizing the city of Brest.*

OPPOSITE BELOW: *The Palais-Bourbon on the left bank.*

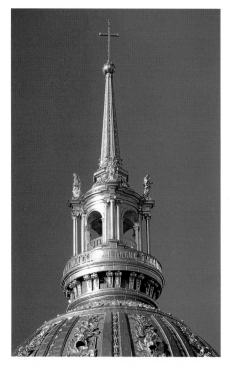

The plight of aged and infirm ex-soldiers had troubled the kings of France from early times and it was Louis XIV who took steps to resolve the problem by building an Hôtel for 4,000 invalids. 'The greatest thought of my reign' he claimed. The architect Libéral Bruant was appointed in 1671 and in 1674 the Hôtel des Invalides was ready to receive its first pensioners. After Bruant's premature death, Mansart carried on the work. The centre of the façade has a large arch over a bas-relief of Louis XIV mounted and in Roman dress. Mutilated during the Revolution, it was restored in 1815.

Today the Invalides houses the fascinating Army Museum and the tombs of military heroes. The two churches built here are both dedicated to St Louis. The first, the soldiers' church, is the work of Bruant and is classical and austere. The second, surmounted by the dome, is Mansart's Baroque masterpiece. The Cour d'Honneur, Court of Honour, is a superb example of Bruant's work, a place of ceremonial parades. It was here that Churchill was kissed by de Gaulle, and here that Dreyfus was publicly disgraced.

LEFT: *The dome of the second of the two churches of the Invalides was added by Mansart in 1706. Of lead sheet over a wooden frame and with intricate gilded decoration, it is one of the outstanding landmarks of Paris.*

RIGHT: *Serene at dawn, the Pont Alexandre III strides across the Seine in a single span 109 metres (358 feet) long and 40 metres (130 feet) wide. Its low profile was designed to preserve the view of the Invalides.*

LEFT: *The Eglise du Dôme on the southern side of the Invalides houses tombs of heroes of France, most notably that of Napoleon himself. His body was returned from St Helena in 1840.*

BELOW: *The morning sun highlights the huge, gilded bronze equestrian statues that flank the Pont Alexandre III.*

LEFT: *The bridge is lavishly decorated in a style that epitomizes the Belle Epoque, the 'Beautiful Age'. The craftsmanship in cast iron is superb. The bridge was built for the exhibition of 1900.*

ABOVE: *Sheltered from the rush of traffic on the Avenue de New York, a lady reclines outside the Palais de Tokyo.*

RIGHT: *The Pont de l'Alma is a modern structure, but, close to the right bank, facing upstream, is the 19th-century statue of a Zouave, a French soldier of the African army corps. In time of flood the severity of the event is marked by the level the waters have reached; frequently his feet, rarely his chest, once, in 1910, up to his chin.*

The American Church in Paris (1927–31) stands on the Quai d'Orsay, which was built in the early 18th century and enlarged a hundred years later by incorporating the little island, l'Ile des Cygnes, where the bodies of the slain were gathered after the St Bartholomew Massacre. In the 16th century it was known as the Ile Maquerelle, a corruption of 'mâle-querelle', manly quarrel, as it was much frequented by duellists. In 1676 Louis XIV decided to colonise the island with swans obtained from Denmark and Sweden, and the new name followed.

The Palais de Tokyo houses the Museum of Modern Art of the City of Paris, the national collections being found at the Musée d'Orsay and the Pompidou Centre. The major schools of 20th century art are represented here, including works by Matisse, Picasso, Braque, Rouault, Utrillo, Suzanne Valadon, Modigliani and Chagall. The largest painting in the world, so it is said, is here: The *Fée Electricité* (Fairy Electricity) by Dufy.

ABOVE LEFT: *A café in the Place de l'Alma provides welcome rest and refreshment.*

ABOVE RIGHT: *On the Place de l'Alma on the right bank stands the memorial to the fighters of the Resistance in the Second World War. Seen from the west the prospect of the Avenue Montaigne leads the eye to the lofty Sacré-Coeur.*

LEFT: *The Palais de Tokyo was built for the World Exhibition of 1937. Impressive but not overpowering; a fine example of monumental architecture.*

ABOVE: *The Eiffel Tower, the Pont d'Iéna and the Avenue du Président Kennedy on the right bank seen from the Pont de Bir-Hakeim.*

RIGHT: *One of the great night views, the Eiffel Tower and the illuminated fountains of the Trocadero Gardens from the Palais de Chaillot. Beyond is the Ecole Militaire and to the left the dome of the Invalides.*

The Quai Branly on the left bank is dominated by the Eiffel Tower. The 1889 Exhibition was to celebrate the centenary of the fall of the Bastille, and in 26 months a mere 200 workers created Gustave Eiffel's masterpiece. The construction cost was 7.5 million francs; the entry fees in the first year totalled 6 million.

The Eiffel Tower is 318 metres (1,043 feet) high and weighs some 7,000 tons. It is said that if it were squashed flat within the area bounded by its feet it would be only 9 cm (3½ inches) high and that the cylinder of air of the same height on the same base weighs more than the Tower itself. But these statistics pale into insignificance alongside the fact that it is the most famous structure in the world; a beloved symbol of Paris.

LEFT: *The Champ-de-Mars, field of Mars, was originally a parade ground, and then a public meeting place, between the Military Academy (1772) and the river. Montgolfier's hot-air balloon flew here in 1783. The temporary pavilion erected for the exhibition of 1889 accommodated a banquet for 35,000 mayors; the metal arches of the Galerie des Machines spanned 115 metres (377 feet). Now peaceful gardens prevail beside the formal walks.*

ABOVE: *From the top of the Eiffel Tower the full extent of the Trocadero Gardens can be seen within the embrace of the wings of the Palais de Chaillot.*

RIGHT: *The terrace of the Palais de Chaillot is usually thronged with people – with tourists, entertainers, and sellers of toys and souvenirs. Here, with the dome of the Invalides beyond, a tap-dancer takes up a collection.*

From the Pont d'Iéna the walks and fountains of the Trocadero Gardens rise to the twin wings of the Palais de Chaillot. The hill on which it stands affords a fine view, as it did in the 16th century when Catherine de Medici built herself a country house here, some distance from the city. The name 'Trocadero' was given to the hill in 1827 to commemorate a minor victory in Spain. The present building was erected in 1937 for the Paris Exhibition, and now houses four specialist museums.

The Musée de la Marine presents all aspects of merchant and fighting ships, the highlight being a collection of models of vessels from the earliest times. The Musée de l'Homme is concerned with humankind, with a collection drawn from all over the world, including in particular the Inuit (Eskimos), Islamic Africans, Pacific

BELOW: *The walkway beside the fountains is a perfect roller-skate slalom course.*

LEFT: *A solitary duck rests beneath the figures of metalworkers flanking the monogram of the French Republic on the Pont de Bir-Hakeim.*

BELOW LEFT: *Wederkinch's statue La France Renaissante on the Pont de Bir-Hakeim. The bridge is a two-deck affair; the road below and the metro line above.*

Islanders, native Americans, Aztecs and Maya. The Musée des Monuments Français gives an opportunity to appreciate the evolving styles of architecture and decoration throughout France from the early Romanesque to the end of the 19th century. Finally, the Musée du Cinéma traces the history of the motion picture from its beginnings to the present day, while the film library frequently shows three or four films a day.

The name 'Pont de Bir-Hakeim' recalls the heroic action of the 1st Free French Brigade Group under General Koenig in 1942. As Rommel's troops advanced across North Africa, a defensive line was established west of Tobruk from the sea some 40 miles (75 km) inland to the French positions at Bir Hakeim. Although out-flanked and eventually almost surrounded, they never surrendered.

F rom the Pont de Bir-Hakeim to the Pont de Grenelle the Seine is divided by the Allée des Cygnes, the Swan Walk. This tree-lined bank only 11 metres (36 feet) wide, was created in 1825 as protection for the Port de Grenelle on the left bank, main river traffic keeping to the northerly channel leaving room for barges to manoeuvre in and out of the docks. Its name is often confused with the old Ile des Cygnes, which was incorporated into the Quai Branly and Quai d'Orsay.

Downstream of the Pont de Grenelle on the tip of the Allée des Cygnes stands the 'miniature' of the Statue of Liberty, presented to the City of Paris by its American community. It is said that until 1937 it faced upstream, towards the bridge, because the President of the Republic in 1886 refused to inaugurate it from a boat.

The left bank no longer has an industrial air. Above and below the Pont de Grenelle the 'Front de Seine', a complex of modern apartment buildings, hotels and shopping plazas, has arisen where the Citroën factory once stood.

ABOVE: *The Maison de Radio-France was built in 1963 to house the Paris offices of the French broadcasting service. The numerous studios are still used for programme production.*

LEFT: *The Allée des Cygnes, where Parisians can 'faire du footing' (go jogging), eat a lunchtime picnic, or just sit in the sun and watch the boats go by.*

OPPOSITE: *The Statue of Liberty, a copy of Bartholdi's original, perhaps feels at home against the Manhattan-style background of the Front de Seine.*

PARIS
GUIDE ALONG THE SEINE

'*Paris is the only city, I think, in which a great river has been used, for mile after mile, on right bank and left, as the natural centre of a work of art.*' So says John Russell, and all who know and love Paris must agree.

From the Pont Sully and the Ile St Louis in the east to the Pont de Grenelle and the Statue of Liberty in the west, by way of Notre-Dame, the Louvre and the Eiffel Tower, this guide, illustrated in full colour, introduces all the major attractions along the Seine and many lesser-known delights as well.

The map helps to choose where you go and how – by foot, boat, bus or train. Both for an hour's boat-cruise and a week's exploration *Paris: Guide Along the Seine* is the ideal companion and souvenir.

Pitkin Guides are a series of high-quality colour souvenir guidebooks to major tourist sites, particularly cathedrals, palaces and historic cities. They are available by mail order – contact Pitkin at this address: Pitkin Pictorials Ltd, Healey House, Dene Road, Andover, Hants SP10 2AA, UK. Tel: 0264 334303 Fax: 0264 334110

Distributed in France by Les Editions du Buot, 30 rue du Rendez-vous, F 75012 Paris, Tel: (1) 43 43 59 03 Fax: (1) 43 45 32 56
Photography: Jean-Loup Princelle. Additional photography: Martin Marix Evans and Frances Schultz. Illustration p.16 by permission of The Bridgeman Art Library. Cover photograph: Robert Harding Picture Library
Written by Martin Marix Evans
Additional research by Jean Roubinet
Designed by Adrian Hodgkins Design
© Pitkin Pictorials Ltd 1991
Printed in Great Britain by Cedar Colour Ltd, Chandlers Ford, Hants.
ISBN 0 85372 532 2   191/10

P PITKIN

ISBN 0-85372-532-2